D1135657

PHOTOGRAPHY

DUNCAN FRASER

Topics

All the words that appear
in **bold** are explained in the
glossary on page 30.

First published in 1986 by
Wayland (Publishers) Ltd
61 Western Road, Hove
East Sussex BN3 1JD

© Copyright 1986 Wayland (Publishers) Ltd

Phototypeset by
Kalligraphics Ltd, Redhill, Surrey
Printed and bound in Belgium by Casterman S.A.

British Library Cataloguing in Publication Data
Fraser, Duncan
    Photography – Topics Wayland (Publishers)
    1. Photography – History – Juvenile literature
    I. Title   II. Series
    770′.9   TR15

ISBN 0–85078–824–2

Contents

Photography Around Us

Every day of our lives, from the moment we get up until the time we go to bed, we are surrounded by photographs.

Photographs in the daily newspapers bring to life the events and the people who make the headlines.

The morning newspapers use photographs to **illustrate** recent events and show people in the news.

The photographer has made this fruit look delicious by arranging it attractively and lighting it skillfully.

These pictures show what was happening more clearly than words alone. Because we see pictures of them, famous people seem much more familiar to us.

Magazines are full of photographs. They may show the different stages of making something, or how food should look if you follow a recipe properly.

MEALZ ON WHEELZ!

Advertisers use eyecatching photography to attract attention to their products.

Many magazines contain fashion photographs showing what sort of clothes are in the shops, and what they look like when worn by a model.

Photographs often appear in magazines to advertise a particular product. These help to make the magazine more colourful. They are also intended to attract your eye and make you want to buy the product being advertised.

Many of the posters which can be seen on walls and **hoardings** will be taken from photographs. In shops, photographs are often used in the design of packets, either to show what is in the packets or to draw them to our attention by making them more attractive.

If you are planning a holiday, or thinking of buying an expensive item, you may want to look at illustrated brochures. These try to show what a place or product looks like, but because they are also advertisements, they will be shown looking their best. Sometimes photographs will make things look better than they really are.

When you go on holiday you will probably take a camera with you. The photographs you bring home will help you to remember the holiday. Some of them may find a place on your mantelpiece, or you may put them in an album, which will become a picture history of your family.

In school, many of the books we read are illustrated with photographs of people, places or

In order to photograph this tiger, the photographer used a telephoto lens, which makes distant objects appear closer.

The photographer has used special techniques and equipment to show this ordinary plastic medicine spoon in a totally new way.

wildlife, which help to bring the text to life. Sometimes teachers may use photographs in the form of **slides** or a film to help us understand a subject better.

Photography is very much part of our daily lives. It shows us what things look like, helps us to remember the past, is used to make things look more attractive, and makes the world we live in more colourful and interesting.

Cameras and Films

Many different types and sizes of camera are made. The simplest to carry and use are the Disc and 110 cameras. They are also the cheapest cameras on the market.

Disc cameras take flat discs of film about 6 cm (2¼ in) across. The **negatives** are set out in a circle around the edge of the disc.

You can see the negatives in a disc camera set out around the edge of the disc.

***Back, from left to right** – Disc, SLR and Compact cameras. **Front** – 110mm camera.*

Cassettes of film 16 mm (½ in) wide are required for 110 cameras. With these cameras you can really only take colour **prints**, and because the negatives are so small, you cannot expect top quality results.

If you want to take colour slides, colour prints, or black and white pictures, you will need a camera that takes 35 mm film. A Compact camera or a 35 mm **SLR** camera (Single Lens Reflex) are both suitable. You will be able to get better quality pictures from these cameras.

Compact cameras are light, easy to carry, and simple to use. Although more expensive than the Disc or 110 cameras, they are very popular and over three-quarters of a million are sold every year. However, the SLR camera is probably the most popular camera in use today, both with amateur

This cross section of a SLR camera shows how complicated cameras have become.

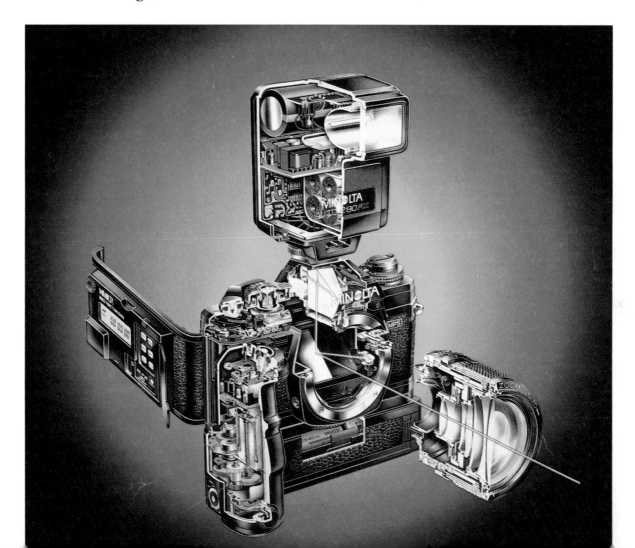

A fisheye lens has an extremely wide view. In this photograph of a Japanese garden you can see how the lens has curved the horizon.

and professional photographers. It has two great advantages: first, you view the picture through the **lens** itself, and not through a separate viewfinder, so that the picture you take is exactly what you see before taking it. Second, you can change the lens at any time. A huge range of lenses is available for SLR cameras, from the **'fisheye'** to the **'telephoto'**, allowing many different effects to be achieved.

Although they look complicated,

SLR cameras can be simple to use: many nowadays are entirely automatic. Prices for these cameras range from cheap to very dear.

Larger cameras than the 35 mm types are normally only used by professional photographers, and when very high quality is required.

Finally, there is the Polaroid camera which produces instant prints. These cameras are great fun to use, and certainly save that long wait while your film is being developed and printed. However, although fairly cheap to buy, they are expensive to use, and do not produce very good quality pictures.

Using a telephoto lens, like this, makes distant objects seem closer – particularly useful when photographing wildlife.

The Invention of Photography

No one person invented photography. From the days of the ancient Greeks this invention was developed slowly and by many different people.

The ancient Greeks knew that light passing through a tiny hole in the wall of a windowless room would make, or 'project', a picture of the outside scene on to the wall

A camera obscura. Light passing through a small lens into a windowless room, projects an image of the outside world onto the wall – upside down!

This is one of the earliest photographs in existence – taken by Nicéphore Niépce in 1829.

opposite the hole. Centuries later, Italian painters used such rooms – called **'camera obscura'** – for studying landscapes, but they used a lens instead of a simple hole. Later, they put the lens in a small box, with a ground glass screen at the end opposite the lens. The picture that appeared on this screen could be seen by someone standing behind the box.

In 1727, a German scientist noticed that the chemical called **silver nitrate** went dark in sunlight. People then started trying to make a picture in a camera obscura by using the direct action of light on chemicals. The first person to do that was a Frenchman called Nicéphore Niépce, in 1826. Unfortunately, it took eight hours to form the picture in the camera!

In the 1830s another Frenchman, Louise Daguerre, produced a picture on a metal plate inside a camera.

Daguerre's plate needed to be exposed to the light coming through the lens for only half an hour. This was because he had discovered that certain chemicals could be used to bring out, or **'develop'**, a picture only partly formed in the camera.

Shortly after Daguerre, an Englishman, William Fox Talbot, announced a different method. Fox Talbot used a camera to make a negative on transparent paper, through which **positives** could be printed. When someone discovered

A picture is formed on a metal plate inside this Daguerre camera.

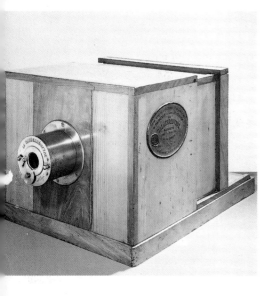

how to use glass for making negatives, Fox Talbot's two stage method became firmly established, and Daguerre's method fell out of use.

About fifty years after Fox Talbot, an American, George Eastman, brought out the first successful roll film, made of a kind of plastic called **celluloid**. It was light, thin, and rolled up neatly on a **spool**. Photographers no longer needed to carry around heavy and fragile glass plates. The age of the snapshot had arrived.

Fox Talbot (on the right of the picture) at work with his assistants. He produced this self-portrait in 1857, using his new paper negative method.

In the century and a half since Niépce took the first photograph, improvements have been made that he could hardly have imagined. Photographs can be taken in one four-thousandth of a second. Film is made that takes pictures by the light of a few candles. Cameras are so small that they can be carried in a pocket or handbag. Some even have tiny computers in them which set the controls automatically. The pleasure of photography is no longer limited to the dedicated few, but is now available to everybody.

Only very modern cameras are capable of capturing a picture like this, of a kingfisher in flight.

Cine Photography

If you look at a strip of *cine film* you will see that it is actually made up of still photographs, each one taken a fraction of a second after the previous one. When shown through a movie projector, the pictures follow one another so quickly that our eyes cannot see them as individual pictures. They merge into each other, and so present what appears as a smooth flowing movement.

The idea of making moving pictures had fascinated people even before the invention of photography. Attempts were made, using painted glass slides and **magic lanterns**, to create an impression of movement by projecting pictures rapidly, one after the other.

Glass, however, was too fragile and bulky to make a moving

This is a toy magic lantern, showing a glass slide in position, ready to be projected.

picture lasting more than a few seconds Even when photography arrived, there was little progress – until Eastman's celluloid film came on to the market. This was the ideal material: strips long enough to take hundreds of pictures could be rolled up on huge spools.

Now people began to look afresh at ways of taking photographs fast

enough to make moving pictures –
which meant taking at least sixteen
pictures every second. Again,
many people helped to solve this
problem, but the first to give a
public showing of a motion picture

*An early movie
projector, showing
the large spools of
film.*

Charlie Chaplin became one of the most famous stars of early cinema.

were two Frenchmen, the Lumière brothers. They demonstrated their *'cinematographe'* in Paris in 1895. Within a few years, 'cinema' had become one of the most popular entertainments the world has ever enjoyed. The addition of sound, in 1927, and colour, in 1935, increased its attraction.

Television, of course, has replaced cinema as a major source of entertainment, and **video cameras** (which work quite differently) are replacing cine cameras, particularly in news reporting. But the 'big screen' still has a special fascination, and will be with us for some time to come.

An American camerawoman at work, filming events to be broadcast on television.

Photography at Work

Some famous photographers make their names by taking photographs of celebrities, or specialize in fashion photography. Certainly, taking portraits of famous people, working on fashion shots for glossy magazines, and producing the pictures that will appear on huge advertising hoardings is the more glamorous side of the work. But it is

The life of a press photographer can be very exciting. Here, photographers record up-to-the-minute news at a press conference in Washington DC.

extremely hard work, and open to only a very few of the thousands of people who make a living as photographers.

The life of a press photographer on a national daily newspaper can be exciting – occasionally even dangerous. But again, only very few people are employed in that kind of work. Being a photographer is more likely to mean working in a studio, attending weddings, taking portraits of people, and sometimes their pets, or providing illustrations for catalogues and local guides.

Some photographers work in hospitals. They are called medical photographers, and their job is to provide photographs for hospital records, research and teaching purposes.

Many photographers work in industry, perhaps taking pictures of industrial processes, or events

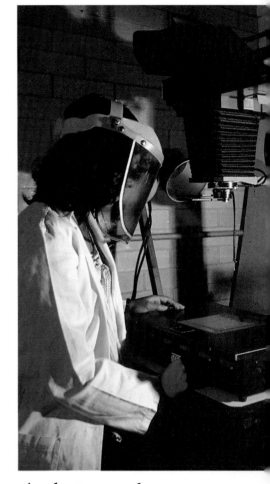

A photographer records the progress of a complicated medical experiment.

A wildlife photographer may travel all over the world. Here, we see a photographer on the Galapogos islands, stalking giant tortoises.

which take place too fast for the human eye to see. Some spend much time photographing wildlife all over the world.

Occasionally pictures may need to be taken through a microscope or a telescope, or even by remote control in situations which might

put a photographer's life in danger. Divers use special underwater cameras to photograph life beneath our lakes and oceans.

The first astronauts on the moon took cameras with them. Many space satellites carry cameras for photographing weather conditions on earth – or for spying on other countries. **Aerial photography** is used for both military and peaceful purposes. For example, it can be

Special cameras are needed for underwater photography, where the sights are spectacular.

This American spacewalker is equipped with two cameras – a stills camera on his back pack and a TV camera on his helmet.

used to check on the position of military bases, and is very useful for map making and for surveying remote areas.

Some policemen are trained as photographers so that they can take photographs of road accidents

and the scenes of crimes. These pictures may be used as evidence in court.

These are just a few of the ways in which cameras are used today. As you have seen, people are using photography in their work or for pleasure all over the world – and beyond.

A photograph of the northwest coastline of Australia, taken by a satellite in space.

Glossary

Aerial Photography Taking photographs from the air.

Camera Obscura Latin for 'a darkened room', even when small boxes were used instead of rooms, the name was kept. It was shortened to 'camera'.

Cassette A light-tight container for film.

Celluloid A kind of transparent plastic.

Developing The treatment of film or photographic paper to bring out the picture.

Fisheye Lens A lens with an extremely wide view – if you placed a camera with a fisheye lens on the floor, pointing it at the ceiling, the picture would include the floor.

Hoarding A large board used for displaying advertisements.

Illustrate To use pictures to show what something looks like.

Lens A piece of glass (or several pieces of glass) shaped so as to form a clear picture at the back of the camera.

Magic Lantern A very early type of slide projector.

Negative A photograph, usually on film, in which the light and dark, and the colour in colour negative, are all the wrong way round.

Positive A photograph, usually on paper, in which the light and dark, and the colour, are the right way round.

Print A photograph on paper, rather than on film.

SLR This stands for 'Single Lens Reflex'; it is a type of camera with one lens and an arrangement of mirrors which reflect the light coming through the lens into the viewfinder.

Silver Nitrate A chemical, made of silver and nitrogen, which turns dark in the light.

Slide A colour film which is projected onto a screen. (Also called a 'transparency'). Photographs made on film.

Spool A device around which film can be wound.

Telephoto Lens A lens which can make distant objects seem closer.

Video Camera A camera which records pictures on a video tape for showing on a television.

Books to Read

A Beginner's Guide to Cameras and Photography by P. Hawksby and J. Chisholm (Usborne Pocketbooks, 1980)

Basic Photography by D. Kilpatrick (Hamlyn, 1984)

The Young Photographer's Pocket Book by J. Dineen (Purnell, 1984)

Instant Picture Handbook by M. Langford (Ebury Press, 1980)

One Touch Photography by J. Partridge (Pan, 1984)

Picture Acknowledgements

Heather Angel 5, 12, 26; BBC Hulton Library 14, 15; Bruce Coleman Limited 13, 18; Duncan Fraser 9, 10; Doug and Anita Lear 20; Minolta II; Photri 23, 24, 28, 29; Planet Earth cover, 27; Science Photo Library 25; Wayland Picture Library 5, 6, 7, 16, 17, 21, 22; Zefa 4.

Index